Can I Ask You A Question, Doctor?

Written by Yasmine Ben Salmi

**The Choice
is Yours**
PUBLISHING

Published by The Choice Is Yours Publishing House

Copyright © 2025 Yasmine Ben Salmi

Copyright © 2025 Ysmine Ben Salmi

Interior and cover design by Lashai Ben Salmi

Paperback ISBN: 978-1-915862-23-5

Hardback ISBN: 978-1-915862-22-8

DEDICATION

Dedication

This book is dedicated to all the aspiring doctors and medical students embarking on this challenging yet rewarding journey, may you find strength in your passion and courage in your doubts.

To the mentors, educators, and healthcare professionals who guide and inspire us every day, thank you for lighting the way.

"To my mentor Dawn Kemp, Director of Museums and Special Collections at the Royal College of Surgeons of England. Thank you for organising my work experience at the Royal College of Surgeons of England."

To my peers and future colleagues, especially those pursuing the demanding path of surgery, may this book remind you that your struggles are shared, your dreams are valid, and your impact is profound.

And to every patient whose stories motivate us to heal and serve with compassion, this book is for you.

May these pages serve as a source of encouragement, hope, and determination as you step boldly into the future of medicine.

Yours sincerely,

Yasmine Ben Salmi

ACKNOWLEDGEMENTS

Acknowledgements

Writing *Can I Ask You a Question, Doctor?* has been a deeply meaningful journey, and I am grateful to all who have supported and inspired me along the way.

Thank you to my family and friends for their unwavering encouragement, patience, and belief in my vision. Your love has been my anchor through every challenge.

I am profoundly grateful to the medical professionals, educators, and mentors both real and fictional, whose experiences and wisdom shaped the voices and stories within this book. Your dedication to healing and teaching fuels the future of medicine.

To my podcast listeners and community, thank you for your trust and engagement. Your stories and questions have continually motivated me to create resources that empower and uplift.

Lastly, to every aspiring doctor reading this book: your commitment to care and learning is vital. It is an honor to share this journey with you.

With heartfelt gratitude,

Yasmine Ben Salmi

INTRODUCTION

Introduction

Becoming a doctor is a journey marked by determination, sacrifice, and an unyielding commitment to care for others. As an aspiring plastic surgeon myself, I know firsthand the challenges and triumphs that come with pursuing a career in medicine. This book, *Can I Ask You a Question, Doctor?*, is inspired by my podcast of the same name, where I have the privilege of engaging with a diverse group of medical professionals, exploring their stories, insights, and lessons learned.

Within these pages, you will meet 20 fictional doctors from different specialties, each representing unique aspects of the UK medical landscape. Their experiences shed light on the realities of medical training, mental health struggles, leadership challenges, and the passion that fuels their commitment to healing and innovation. Through their narratives, I aim to offer inspiration, practical advice, and encouragement to fellow medical students, junior doctors, and anyone interested in the medical field.

This book blends real UK facts and statistics with these fictionalised but authentic voices, providing a rich understanding of the medical profession's current climate. It also integrates my expertise in mental health, wellbeing, mindset, and leadership, reflecting the holistic approach necessary for thriving in this demanding career.

Medicine is not only about science and skill, it's about resilience, empathy, and growth. Each chapter concludes with actionable tips and techniques, designed to empower you to take confident steps in your journey. Whether you are navigating medical school, residency, or simply contemplating a career in healthcare, this book invites you to learn from the experiences of those who have walked the path before you.

As you read, I encourage you to reflect on your own aspirations and challenges. May these stories inspire you to embrace your journey with courage and curiosity, knowing you are part of a community dedicated to healing and leadership.

Welcome to *Can I Ask You a Question, Doctor?*

Let's explore what it truly means to become a doctor.

Yasmine Ben Salmi

TABLE OF CONTENTS

Table of Contents

Dedication page 3
Acknowledgements page 5
Introduction page 7

Chapter 1: Dr. Aisha Patel – The Compassionate General Practitioner page 14

Chapter 2: Dr. Liam Turner – The Resilient Emergency Medicine Physician page 18

Chapter 3: Dr. Olivia Clarke – The Innovative Pediatrician page 22

Chapter 4: Dr. Marcus Bennett – The Determined Psychiatrist page 26

Chapter 5: Dr. Sophie Kim – The Mindful Anaesthetist page 30

Chapter 6: Dr. Ethan Shaw – The Analytical Radiologist page 34

Chapter 7: Dr. Grace Lewis – The Passionate Obstetrician page 38

Chapter 8: Dr. Noah Adams – The Detail-Oriented Pathologist page 42

Chapter 9: Dr. Emma Foster – The Empathetic Oncology Specialist page 46

Chapter 10: Dr. Daniel Hughes – The Inspiring Medical Educator page 50

Chapter 11: Dr. Mia Campbell – The Adaptable Infectious Diseases Consultant page 54

Chapter 12: Dr. Benjamin Ross – The Patient-Centered Cardiologist page 58

Chapter 13: Dr. Hannah Scott – The Visionary Neurologist page 62

Chapter 14: Dr. Samuel Price – The Tenacious Surgeon page 66

Chapter 15: Dr. Zoe Morgan – The Holistic Dermatologist page 70

Chapter 16: Dr. Alex Mitchell – The Supportive Psychiatric Nurse Practitioner page 74

Chapter 17: Dr. Clara Evans – The Driven Research Scientist page 78

Chapter 18: Dr. Jacob Wright – The Collaborative Public Health Physician page 82

Chapter 19: Dr. Isabella Grant – The Compassionate Geriatrician page 86

Chapter 20: Dr. Michael Patel – The Balanced Plastic Surgeon page 90

Bonus Chapter page 94
Affirmations page 98
Conclusion page 141
Final Message page 143
About the Author page 145
Keep in Touch page 148
Notes page 150

CHAPTER 1

Chapter 1: Dr. Aisha Patel – The Compassionate General Practitioner

Dr. Aisha Patel's journey into medicine began in a small community in Birmingham, where she witnessed firsthand the vital role of general practitioners in bridging healthcare gaps. From an early age, she was drawn to the idea of becoming a trusted confidant and healer for people from all walks of life. Her path was marked by challenges, including balancing rigorous academics with family responsibilities, but her unwavering commitment to community health kept her motivated.

During her medical school years, Aisha found herself fascinated by the holistic nature of general practice, the blend of science, empathy, and continuous patient relationships. However, she also encountered the growing pressures faced by GPs in the UK: increasing patient loads, administrative burdens, and limited resources. These realities tested her resilience but reinforced her desire to advocate for better support within the NHS system.

Aisha's approach to medicine centers on compassionate listening and personalised care. She believes that understanding a patient's story beyond symptoms is essential to effective healing. Her daily practice involves navigating complex mental health concerns, chronic illnesses, and social determinants of health, reflecting the multifaceted challenges faced by many GPs today.

Through her experience, Aisha has developed techniques to manage stress and prevent burnout, such as mindfulness, setting healthy boundaries, and seeking peer support. She emphasises the importance of self-care as a foundation for sustaining empathy and high-quality care in demanding environments.

Her story highlights the essential but often overlooked role of general practitioners in the UK's healthcare ecosystem. Despite systemic challenges, Aisha's dedication exemplifies how passion and resilience can transform obstacles into opportunities for meaningful impact.

For aspiring doctors, especially those considering general practice, Aisha's journey offers valuable lessons on balancing personal wellbeing with professional commitment, and the power of compassionate care in improving lives.

Tips & Techniques

- Practice active, empathetic listening in patient interactions.

- Establish clear work-life boundaries to prevent burnout.
- Utilise mindfulness exercises to maintain emotional balance.

Action Steps

1. Reflect on your motivations for pursuing medicine and write a personal mission statement.
2. Explore volunteering opportunities in community health settings to gain exposure to general practice.
3. Develop a daily mindfulness or relaxation routine to support wellbeing.

Key Takeaways

- General practice requires a blend of medical knowledge and deep empathy.
- Resilience and self-care are critical in managing the demands of the profession.
- Understanding patient stories beyond symptoms leads to better outcomes.

CHAPTER 2

Chapter 2: Dr. Liam Turner – The Resilient Emergency Medicine Physician

Dr. Liam Turner's path to emergency medicine was shaped by his love for fast-paced problem-solving and his desire to make an immediate impact. Growing up in Manchester, Liam was inspired by stories of frontline healthcare workers during crises, fueling his ambition to be part of a team that saves lives in urgent situations. His journey, however, was far from smooth, as the emotional toll and physical exhaustion of emergency work tested his limits.

During his foundation years, Liam faced long shifts, unpredictable schedules, and the constant pressure of critical decision-making. The UK's emergency departments often experience overcrowding and resource shortages, factors that amplify the stress on staff. Liam recalls moments when he questioned his stamina and mental toughness, but the support of colleagues and a strong sense of purpose kept him going.

One of the biggest challenges Liam encountered was managing the mental health impacts of witnessing trauma and loss regularly. He emphasises the importance of debriefing sessions, peer support groups, and seeking professional help when needed. Developing resilience wasn't about suppressing emotions but learning to process them constructively.

Liam also highlights the significance of continuous learning in emergency medicine. The specialty demands staying updated with evolving protocols and technologies, requiring dedication beyond clinical hours. Despite the intensity, he finds fulfillment in moments of teamwork and successfully stabilising patients in crisis.

For aspiring doctors considering emergency medicine, Liam's story serves as both a realistic and inspiring guide. It showcases the need for resilience, adaptability, and self-care in a specialty where every second counts and every action can save a life.

Tips & Techniques

- Prioritise regular debriefing and mental health check-ins with your team.
- Develop quick decision-making skills through simulation training.
- Establish routines that support physical and emotional recovery post-shifts.

Action Steps

1. Participate in emergency medicine workshops or shadow shifts to experience the environment.
2. Create a personal resilience plan, including coping strategies and support networks.
3. Practice stress management techniques such as deep breathing or grounding exercises during shifts.

Key Takeaways

- Emergency medicine is demanding but deeply impactful work.
- Resilience stems from acknowledging emotions and seeking support.
- Continuous learning and teamwork are essential for success.

CHAPTER 3

Chapter 3: Dr. Olivia Clarke – The Innovative Pediatrician

Dr. Olivia Clarke's passion for pediatrics was ignited by her early volunteer work in children's hospitals across London. She was drawn to the unique challenges of caring for young patients, whose needs require not only medical expertise but also sensitivity to family dynamics and developmental stages. Olivia's journey reflects both the joys and complexities of working in child health within the UK's NHS system.

Throughout medical school and her pediatric training, Olivia became fascinated by the potential of technology and innovation to improve pediatric care. From telemedicine to personalised treatment plans, she embraces advances that increase access and improve outcomes for children, especially those in underserved communities. Yet, she also encountered systemic hurdles such as funding constraints and workforce shortages that limit the scope of such innovations.

Olivia's practice emphasises family-centered care, involving parents and caregivers as active partners. She believes that understanding the child's environment and emotional wellbeing is crucial to successful treatment and long-term health. This holistic approach helps her navigate cases ranging from chronic illnesses to acute emergencies.

Balancing professional demands with personal wellbeing has been vital for Olivia. She advocates for peer mentorship programs and professional development opportunities that foster growth and prevent burnout. Her story underscores the importance of innovation combined with empathy in pediatric medicine.

For aspiring pediatricians, Olivia's journey offers encouragement to remain adaptable, compassionate, and forward-thinking in a field that continually evolves to meet children's diverse needs.

Tips & Techniques

- Engage families in care discussions to build trust and improve adherence.
- Stay updated with emerging pediatric technologies and research.
- Seek out mentorship and peer support to navigate challenges.

Action Steps

1. Volunteer or shadow in pediatric settings to understand the specialty's demands.

2. Identify one area of pediatric care where innovation could improve outcomes and research it.
3. Connect with a mentor to support your personal and professional development.

Key Takeaways

- Pediatric care requires medical skill and emotional intelligence.
- Innovation and empathy together enhance child health outcomes.
- Mentorship and ongoing learning are essential for career sustainability.

CHAPTER 4

Chapter 4: Dr. Marcus Bennett – The Determined Psychiatrist

Dr. Marcus Bennett's journey into psychiatry began with a deep desire to understand the complexities of the human mind and help those struggling with mental health. Raised in Liverpool, Marcus witnessed the stigma surrounding mental illness in his community, fueling his commitment to change perceptions and provide compassionate care. His path to becoming a psychiatrist was marked by challenges including confronting his own biases and navigating a demanding training pathway.

Throughout his studies and clinical rotations, Marcus was struck by the growing prevalence of mental health conditions in the UK, with one in four people experiencing a mental health problem each year. He recognised that despite advances, access to timely and effective psychiatric care remains a significant challenge. These realities motivated him to advocate for integrated care models that combine physical and mental health services.

Marcus's practice emphasises patient-centered care, tailoring treatment plans that respect each individual's story and cultural background. He works closely with multidisciplinary teams to address not only symptoms but also social determinants like housing and employment, which profoundly impact mental wellbeing.

To sustain his own mental health, Marcus adopts techniques such as reflective journaling, peer supervision, and mindfulness meditation. He highlights the importance of breaking down stigma within the medical profession to create environments where clinicians feel supported.

For aspiring psychiatrists, Marcus's story illustrates the importance of resilience, empathy, and advocacy. His experience shows that mental health care requires not just medical expertise but also courage to challenge societal barriers.

Tips & Techniques

- Practice active listening and validate patients' experiences without judgment.
- Incorporate holistic approaches that address social and environmental factors.
- Use reflective practices to process emotional challenges in your work.

Action Steps

1. Engage with mental health awareness programs to deepen understanding of stigma.

2. Explore multidisciplinary teamwork in clinical placements.
3. Develop a personal self-care plan including mindfulness or journaling.

Key Takeaways

- Psychiatry combines medical knowledge with empathy and advocacy.
- Addressing social factors is key to effective mental health care.
- Self-care and reflection are vital for sustainability in the field.

CHAPTER 5

Chapter 5: Dr. Sophie Kim – The Mindful Anaesthetist

Dr. Sophie Kim's fascination with anaesthesia stemmed from her love of physiology and the critical role anaesthetists play in patient safety during surgery. Training in London, Sophie quickly learned that the specialty demands not only technical precision but also calmness under pressure. Her journey highlighted the intense responsibility of ensuring patients' wellbeing while they are unconscious and vulnerable.

Anaesthetists in the UK face unique challenges, including high-stakes decision-making and working closely with surgical teams in fast-paced environments. Sophie emphasises the importance of mindfulness, being fully present in the moment, to reduce errors and maintain focus. This practice has helped her manage the stresses of her role and improve patient outcomes.

Beyond the operating theatre, Sophie advocates for better awareness of anaesthetists' wellbeing. The specialty is often overlooked in discussions about clinician burnout, despite long hours and emotional demands. She encourages peers to build supportive networks and prioritise mental health alongside professional development.

Sophie's approach integrates self-care, mindfulness training, and teamwork, demonstrating how a mindful mindset enhances both clinical performance and personal resilience. Her story offers valuable insights for anyone considering this critical yet sometimes underappreciated specialty.

For aspiring doctors interested in anaesthesia, Sophie's journey underscores the balance of scientific expertise and emotional regulation needed to thrive.

Tips & Techniques

- Practice mindfulness meditation to enhance focus and reduce stress.
- Develop strong communication skills for effective teamwork in the operating room.
- Schedule regular self-care routines to prevent burnout.

Action Steps

1. Explore mindfulness resources tailored for healthcare professionals.
2. Seek opportunities to shadow anaesthetists and observe their workflow.
3. Join or form peer support groups focused on wellbeing in high-pressure specialties.

Key Takeaways

- Anaesthesia requires technical skill combined with emotional calmness.
- Mindfulness improves focus and reduces clinical errors.
- Prioritising mental health is essential in demanding medical roles.

CHAPTER 6

Chapter 6: Dr. Ethan Shaw – The Analytical Radiologist

Dr. Ethan Shaw's interest in radiology was sparked by his fascination with medical imaging and the power of technology to reveal hidden diagnoses. Growing up in Edinburgh, he was captivated by the blend of cutting-edge science and detective work involved in interpreting scans. His journey through medical school and specialty training revealed both the exciting advancements and the unique challenges faced by radiologists in the UK.

Radiology is often described as a "behind-the-scenes" specialty, where doctors provide critical insights that guide patient care without direct patient contact. Ethan found this aspect both rewarding and isolating. UK radiologists face increasing workloads due to rising imaging demand and a shortage of specialists, leading to pressure to maintain accuracy under time constraints.

To manage these demands, Ethan developed techniques to enhance concentration and minimise errors, such as structured reporting, double reading, and regular breaks. He also emphasises the importance of ongoing education to keep pace with rapidly evolving imaging technologies, including AI integration.

Despite the challenges, Ethan's work allows him to contribute meaningfully to diagnoses and treatment decisions, often saving lives with early detection. He encourages aspiring radiologists to cultivate analytical thinking, attention to detail, and a passion for lifelong learning.

His story highlights the vital role of radiology in modern medicine and the resilience needed to thrive amid evolving technology and healthcare demands.

Tips & Techniques

- Use structured reporting to improve clarity and reduce errors.
- Incorporate regular breaks to maintain focus during high workloads.
- Stay updated with new imaging technologies and AI applications.

Action Steps

1. Shadow a radiologist to observe diagnostic processes firsthand.
2. Practice interpreting sample imaging reports to develop analytical skills.
3. Join professional forums or attend workshops on radiology advancements.

Key Takeaways

- Radiology combines technology and detective work essential for diagnosis.
- Managing workload and continuous learning are key challenges.
- Analytical skills and attention to detail are crucial for success.

CHAPTER 7

Chapter 7: Dr. Grace Lewis – The Passionate Obstetrician

Dr. Grace Lewis's calling to obstetrics began during her early clinical placements when she witnessed the profound joy and vulnerability that accompany childbirth. Raised in Cardiff, Grace was inspired by the opportunity to support women and families through one of life's most transformative experiences. Her journey into obstetrics was shaped by both exhilarating successes and heart-wrenching challenges.

Obstetricians in the UK play a critical role in ensuring safe pregnancies and deliveries, yet the specialty faces growing pressures. Rising maternal age, obesity rates, and socioeconomic disparities contribute to complex cases, increasing demands on healthcare providers. Grace recalls moments when the balance between technology and personalised care became crucial to positive outcomes.

Throughout her training, Grace learned to navigate these complexities with empathy and skill, often acting as both a medical expert and emotional support for her patients. She stresses the importance of communication, teamwork, and cultural sensitivity in obstetric care, particularly when managing high-risk pregnancies.

To maintain her wellbeing amid the pressures of the specialty, Grace practices regular exercise, mindfulness, and seeks mentorship from senior colleagues. She encourages aspiring obstetricians to build resilience and cultivate a supportive network.

Grace's story exemplifies the passion and dedication required to excel in obstetrics, a specialty that blends science, emotion, and leadership in equal measure.

Tips & Techniques

- Develop clear, compassionate communication skills for patient interactions.
- Stay informed about current guidelines on maternal health and risk management.
- Build a strong professional support system to navigate challenges.

Action Steps

1. Volunteer or shadow in maternity wards to gain firsthand experience.
2. Study case reviews on high-risk pregnancies to understand complex scenarios.
3. Identify a mentor in obstetrics to guide your career development.

Key Takeaways

- Obstetrics demands a blend of medical expertise and empathetic care.
- Communication and teamwork are vital in managing complex cases.
- Resilience and mentorship support long-term success.

CHAPTER 8

Chapter 8: Dr. Noah Adams – The Detail-Oriented Pathologist

Dr. Noah Adams's fascination with pathology started during his preclinical years when he realised the profound impact of microscopic analysis on patient diagnosis. Growing up in Newcastle, he was drawn to the precision and investigative nature of pathology, often called the "hidden science" of medicine. Noah's journey reveals the importance of meticulous attention to detail and the vital, yet often unseen, role pathologists play in healthcare.

Pathology in the UK faces challenges such as increasing demand for diagnostic services, limited workforce capacity, and the pressure to maintain rapid turnaround times without compromising accuracy. Noah experienced firsthand the balancing act between thoroughness and efficiency, recognising that errors can have far-reaching consequences for patient care.

To excel, Noah developed disciplined work habits, including checklists, double verification, and continuous quality improvement measures. He also embraced new technologies like digital pathology and AI-assisted diagnostics, which promise to transform the field and improve patient outcomes.

Noah's role requires a deep commitment to continuous learning and collaboration with clinical teams to ensure diagnostic findings translate into effective treatment plans. His experience underscores how pathologists are central to the medical team, providing the foundation for many clinical decisions.

For aspiring pathologists, Noah's story highlights the value of precision, patience, and embracing innovation while understanding the critical impact of their work behind the scenes.

Tips & Techniques

- Use systematic checklists to reduce errors and improve consistency.
- Stay abreast of emerging diagnostic technologies and digital tools.
- Foster communication with clinical teams to contextualise findings.

Action Steps

1. Seek opportunities to observe pathology labs to understand workflow and challenges.
2. Practice detailed case reviews to sharpen diagnostic reasoning.
3. Join professional pathology societies to access resources and networking.

Key Takeaways

- Pathology is a detail-driven specialty essential to accurate diagnosis.
- Balancing efficiency with precision is a critical skill.
- Collaboration and technology adoption enhance patient care.

CHAPTER 9

Chapter 9: Dr. Emma Foster – The Empathetic Oncology Specialist

Dr. Emma Foster's dedication to oncology emerged from a personal experience, losing a family member to cancer, instilling in her a deep compassion for patients facing life-changing diagnoses. Training in London, Emma encountered the emotional complexities of oncology: balancing hope and realism while supporting patients through treatment and survivorship.

The UK's oncology landscape is evolving, with advancements in targeted therapies and immunotherapies offering new hope. However, challenges such as long waiting times, funding limitations, and emotional burnout among healthcare professionals persist. Emma learned that oncology requires not only scientific expertise but also resilience and emotional intelligence.

Emma's practice focuses on patient-centered care, ensuring that each individual's values and preferences shape treatment plans. She works closely with multidisciplinary teams, including nurses, social workers, and psychologists, to provide holistic support addressing physical, emotional, and social needs.

To sustain her own wellbeing, Emma uses techniques such as reflective supervision, peer support, and maintaining hobbies outside work. She stresses the importance of acknowledging grief and celebrating small victories in the cancer journey.

For aspiring oncologists, Emma's story offers insight into the blend of science, empathy, and resilience needed to navigate this demanding yet rewarding specialty.

Tips & Techniques

- Develop strong communication skills to discuss prognosis and treatment options compassionately.
- Engage in multidisciplinary collaboration to address patient needs holistically.
- Practice self-reflection and seek peer support to manage emotional challenges.

Action Steps

1. Volunteer in oncology wards or support groups to understand patient experiences.
2. Attend workshops on communication skills for delivering difficult news.
3. Establish personal routines that promote emotional wellbeing outside work.

Key Takeaways

- Oncology combines cutting-edge science with deep empathy.
- Teamwork and holistic care improve patient outcomes.
- Emotional resilience is vital for healthcare providers in this field.

CHAPTER 10

Chapter 10: Dr. Amina Patel – The Compassionate General Practitioner

Dr. Amina Patel's journey into general practice was driven by her passion for holistic, community-centered healthcare. Growing up in Birmingham, she saw firsthand how social determinants like housing, education, and income influence health outcomes. This inspired her to become a GP, a specialty at the heart of the UK's NHS, serving as the first point of contact for millions.

Amina's training exposed her to the broad scope of general practice, from managing chronic diseases to addressing mental health and preventative care. She encountered challenges such as patient demand exceeding available appointments and the complexity of multimorbidity, where patients suffer from multiple long-term conditions.

Her approach focuses on building long-term relationships with patients, empowering them to take charge of their health. Amina emphasises listening actively, understanding cultural contexts, and promoting self-care strategies that fit individual lifestyles.

To manage the pressures of her role, Amina emphasises work-life balance and advocates for team-based care models that include nurses, pharmacists, and social workers to improve patient support.

For aspiring doctors, Amina's story illustrates the rewarding, diverse nature of general practice and its pivotal role in the healthcare system.

Tips & Techniques

- Develop strong communication and interpersonal skills for diverse patient interactions.
- Learn to manage time effectively to balance clinical and administrative duties.
- Promote patient education and self-care as key components of treatment.

Action Steps

1. Volunteer in community health clinics to gain exposure to primary care.
2. Practice patient-centered communication techniques in clinical settings.
3. Explore team-based care models and how they improve patient outcomes.

Key Takeaways

- General practice demands broad medical knowledge and empathy.
- Building patient relationships is central to effective care.
- Teamwork and self-care promote sustainable practice.

CHAPTER 11

Chapter 11: Dr. Samuel Hayes – The Trailblazing Cardiologist

Dr. Samuel Hayes's passion for cardiology was ignited during a medical elective in Glasgow, where he witnessed the life-saving impact of cardiac interventions. Raised in a working-class family, Samuel was motivated to address the growing burden of cardiovascular disease in the UK, which remains the leading cause of death nationwide.

Throughout his rigorous training, Samuel confronted challenges such as keeping pace with rapid advances in interventional cardiology and managing patients with complex comorbidities like diabetes and obesity. The pressure to deliver high-quality care in an overstretched NHS system tested his perseverance and adaptability.

Samuel emphasises the importance of prevention and patient education, encouraging lifestyle changes alongside medical treatment. He advocates for incorporating digital health tools to monitor heart health remotely, improving patient engagement and outcomes.

To maintain resilience, Samuel practices physical fitness, mentors junior doctors, and participates in research to contribute to innovations in cardiology.

His story illustrates how combining clinical expertise with leadership and advocacy can drive meaningful change.

For aspiring cardiologists, Samuel's journey offers inspiration to embrace lifelong learning and the potential to impact population health through both individual care and public health initiatives.

Tips & Techniques

- Stay current with clinical guidelines and emerging cardiac technologies.
- Foster patient-centered communication emphasising prevention.
- Balance clinical duties with research and mentorship for growth.

Action Steps

1. Shadow cardiologists in various subspecialties to explore interests.
2. Engage in community health projects focused on cardiovascular risk reduction.
3. Develop a personal fitness routine to model healthy lifestyle habits.

Key Takeaways

- Cardiology requires technical skill, prevention focus, and adaptability.
- Patient education is critical in managing chronic heart disease.
- Leadership and research complement clinical practice.

CHAPTER 12

Chapter 12: Dr. Layla Hassan – The Visionary Neurologist

Dr. Layla Hassan's fascination with the nervous system began during her neuroscience studies at university. Born and raised in Manchester, Layla was inspired by the complexity of the brain and its influence on every aspect of human function. Her journey into neurology has been marked by both awe for medical science and a commitment to improving patient quality of life.

Neurology presents unique challenges in the UK healthcare system, including long waiting lists for specialist appointments and the intricacies of diagnosing often subtle and overlapping neurological conditions. Layla highlights the importance of thorough clinical assessment combined with advances in neuroimaging and biomarkers to improve diagnostic accuracy.

Her practice is patient-focused, emphasizing clear communication to help patients and families understand complex conditions like multiple sclerosis, epilepsy, and Parkinson's disease. She collaborates closely with therapists and support groups to provide comprehensive care beyond medication.

To prevent burnout, Layla practices regular physical activity, mindfulness, and actively seeks professional development opportunities. She believes that curiosity and compassion are essential for neurologists facing both medical uncertainty and emotional complexity.

For aspiring neurologists, Layla's story encourages embracing complexity with resilience and a multidisciplinary approach to patient care.

Tips & Techniques

- Master detailed neurological examination skills to aid diagnosis.
- Use patient-friendly language to explain complex neurological conditions.
- Collaborate with multidisciplinary teams for holistic care.

Action Steps

1. Observe neurological clinics to gain exposure to patient assessment.
2. Study common neurological disorders and their presentations.
3. Engage in mindfulness or stress-management techniques.

Key Takeaways

- Neurology demands scientific rigor and compassionate communication.
- Multidisciplinary care improves patient outcomes.
- Resilience is vital in managing diagnostic uncertainty.

CHAPTER 13

Chapter 13: Dr. Olivia Reed – The Dedicated Paediatrician

Dr. Olivia Reed's passion for paediatrics grew from her love of working with children and a desire to make a difference during the most formative years of life. Raised in Bristol, Olivia saw how early health interventions can shape lifelong wellbeing and was inspired to pursue a specialty that blends medical care with advocacy for vulnerable young patients.

Paediatrics in the UK presents unique challenges, including managing complex chronic conditions, addressing health inequalities, and communicating effectively with both children and their families. Olivia emphasises that paediatricians must be adaptable, compassionate, and skilled in building trust with young patients.

Her work involves coordinating care across multiple specialties and collaborating with schools, social services, and community organisations to support holistic child health. Olivia also prioritises educating parents about self-care strategies and developmental milestones.

To maintain her own wellbeing, Olivia practices work-life balance through hobbies and mindfulness, and she participates in peer support networks tailored for paediatric professionals. She encourages aspiring paediatricians to nurture patience and empathy alongside clinical skills.

Olivia's story highlights the rewarding yet demanding nature of paediatrics, a specialty requiring dedication to the wellbeing of children and their families.

Tips & Techniques

- Develop child-friendly communication strategies to build rapport.
- Stay informed on guidelines for managing chronic paediatric conditions.
- Collaborate with multidisciplinary teams including social workers and educators.

Action Steps

1. Volunteer in paediatric wards or clinics to gain practical experience.
2. Study common paediatric illnesses and developmental psychology.
3. Join paediatric professional groups or forums for networking and support.

Key Takeaways

- Paediatrics combines medical expertise with advocacy and empathy.
- Effective communication with children and families is essential.
- Multidisciplinary collaboration enhances holistic care.

CHAPTER 14

Chapter 14: Dr. Marcus Bennett – The Innovative Emergency Medicine Consultant

Dr. Marcus Bennett's passion for emergency medicine was sparked by the fast-paced, high-impact nature of urgent care. Growing up in Leeds, Marcus was drawn to the challenge of making rapid, life-saving decisions and the variety of cases seen in the emergency department (ED). His journey through training highlighted the need for resilience, teamwork, and adaptability.

Emergency medicine in the UK faces significant pressures, including overcrowded departments, resource constraints, and managing diverse patient presentations ranging from minor injuries to critical trauma. Marcus emphasises the importance of staying calm under pressure and developing strong clinical prioritisation skills.

Marcus also advocates for innovations such as simulation training and improved triage protocols to enhance patient safety and staff preparedness. He highlights the value of leadership and communication skills in coordinating multidisciplinary teams during emergencies.

To sustain his own wellbeing, Marcus uses physical exercise, debrief sessions, and maintains a supportive professional network. He encourages aspiring emergency physicians to develop mental toughness and embrace continuous learning.

His story illustrates how emergency medicine is a demanding but profoundly rewarding specialty that requires quick thinking, compassion, and collaboration.

Tips & Techniques

- Practice simulation scenarios to improve emergency response skills.
- Develop strong prioritisation and multitasking abilities.
- Engage in regular debriefing and peer support to process challenging cases.

Action Steps

1. Volunteer in an emergency department to observe workflow and pressures.
2. Learn about triage systems and protocols in urgent care.
3. Build physical and mental resilience through fitness and mindfulness.

Key Takeaways

- Emergency medicine demands rapid decision-making and resilience.
- Simulation and teamwork improve patient outcomes.
- Self-care and peer support are vital for sustainability.

CHAPTER 15

Chapter 15: Dr. Zara Khan – The Passionate Psychiatrist

Dr. Zara Khan's dedication to psychiatry grew from her deep desire to understand the human mind and support those struggling with mental health challenges. Raised in London, Zara saw the stigma around mental illness and became determined to change perceptions and improve care within the NHS.

Psychiatry in the UK faces ongoing challenges including resource shortages, long waiting times for patients, and balancing medication with therapy approaches. Zara emphasises the importance of listening with empathy and creating a non-judgmental space for patients to share their experiences.

Her practice integrates psychological therapies, medication, and social support, working closely with community teams to provide comprehensive mental health care. Zara also advocates for public awareness campaigns to reduce stigma and encourage early intervention.

To protect her own mental wellbeing, Zara practices mindfulness, engages in regular supervision, and promotes a healthy work-life balance. She encourages aspiring psychiatrists to develop emotional resilience and cultural competence.

Zara's story illustrates psychiatry's vital role in holistic health and the courage required to support patients through complex emotional journeys.

Tips & Techniques

- Cultivate active listening and empathy in patient interactions.
- Stay updated on evidence-based psychotherapies and pharmacological treatments.
- Participate in peer supervision and reflective practice.

Action Steps

1. Volunteer with mental health charities to understand patient perspectives.
2. Attend workshops on communication skills in psychiatry.
3. Develop personal strategies for stress management and self-care.

Key Takeaways

- Psychiatry blends medical treatment with compassionate care.
- Reducing stigma is essential for improving mental health access.
- Emotional resilience supports sustainable practice.

CHAPTER 16

Chapter 16: Dr. Ethan Clark – The Meticulous Radiologist

Dr. Ethan Clark's fascination with radiology began when he realized how imaging technology transforms diagnosis and treatment plans. Growing up in Edinburgh, he admired how radiologists serve as the eyes behind the scenes, interpreting images to guide patient care.

Radiology in the UK faces growing demand due to an aging population and technological advancements like MRI, CT scans, and ultrasound. Ethan highlights the importance of precision and continuous learning, given the rapid evolution of imaging techniques and the challenge of balancing workload with accuracy.

His daily work involves collaborating closely with clinicians, ensuring timely and accurate reports that influence surgical decisions, cancer treatments, and emergency care. Ethan emphasises developing strong analytical skills and embracing new tools like AI-assisted diagnostics to enhance practice.

To avoid burnout, Ethan maintains a strict work-life balance, engages in teaching, and participates in multidisciplinary team meetings. His journey underscores radiology as a specialty where curiosity, detail orientation, and communication converge.

For aspiring radiologists, Ethan's story inspires embracing technology alongside clinical insight to improve patient outcomes.

Tips & Techniques

- Develop keen observational and analytical skills for image interpretation.
- Stay updated with emerging radiology technologies and protocols.
- Foster clear communication with multidisciplinary teams.

Action Steps

1. Seek shadowing opportunities in radiology departments.
2. Practice interpreting sample imaging cases.
3. Engage with professional radiology societies and continuing education.

Key Takeaways

- Radiology is critical to accurate diagnosis and treatment planning.
- Technological advances require ongoing learning and adaptation.
- Collaboration with clinicians enhances patient care.

CHAPTER 17

Chapter 17: Dr. Isabella Morgan – The Compassionate Obstetrician and Gynaecologist

Dr. Isabella Morgan's passion for obstetrics and gynaecology was sparked by her desire to support women through some of the most profound moments of their lives from childbirth to managing reproductive health. Raised in Cardiff, Isabella was inspired by the blend of surgical skill and compassionate care required in her field.

In the UK, obstetrics and gynaecology faces challenges such as rising maternal age, increasing rates of complex pregnancies, and addressing health disparities among different populations. Isabella emphasises the importance of personalised care, listening to patients' preferences, and advocating for informed decision-making.

Her work spans antenatal clinics, labour wards, and surgical theatres, requiring technical proficiency and emotional resilience. Isabella collaborates closely with midwives, paediatricians, and mental health teams to ensure comprehensive care.

To maintain her wellbeing, she practices mindfulness, seeks peer support, and balances her demanding schedule with family time. Isabella encourages aspiring OBGYNs to develop strong communication skills and embrace continuous professional development.

Her story highlights the rewarding and challenging nature of a specialty dedicated to women's health and life's milestones.

Tips & Techniques

- Build empathetic communication to support women through sensitive experiences.
- Stay current with guidelines on maternal and reproductive health.
- Develop teamwork skills with multidisciplinary maternity care teams.

Action Steps

1. Volunteer in maternity units or women's health clinics.
2. Study key conditions in obstetrics and gynaecology.
3. Attend workshops on patient-centred care and communication.

Key Takeaways

- OBGYN requires a blend of surgical skill and empathy.
- Personalised, holistic care improves outcomes and patient satisfaction.
- Continuous learning is essential in this evolving field.

CHAPTER 18

Chapter 18: Dr. Michael Evans – The Committed Rheumatologist

Dr. Michael Evans's interest in rheumatology was piqued during his clinical rotations when he encountered patients suffering from chronic, often debilitating musculoskeletal conditions. Raised in Cardiff, Michael was drawn to the challenge of managing complex autoimmune diseases and improving patients' quality of life through both medication and lifestyle interventions.

Rheumatology in the UK faces the challenge of managing long-term conditions such as rheumatoid arthritis, lupus, and osteoarthritis within an overstretched NHS. Michael emphasises the importance of early diagnosis and multidisciplinary care, combining pharmacological treatment with physiotherapy and occupational therapy.

He advocates for patient education and self-management strategies, empowering individuals to take an active role in their health. Michael collaborates closely with primary care, therapists, and social services to provide comprehensive support.

To maintain his own wellbeing, Michael emphasises regular exercise, maintains a healthy work-life balance, and participates in rheumatology research to stay at the forefront of advances.

His journey underscores the rewarding impact of rheumatology on patients' lives through ongoing care and innovation.

Tips & Techniques

- Develop thorough clinical assessment skills for musculoskeletal conditions.
- Promote patient education and self-management techniques.
- Collaborate with multidisciplinary teams for holistic care.

Action Steps

1. Volunteer in rheumatology clinics to gain exposure.
2. Study common autoimmune diseases and treatment options.
3. Attend professional development courses focused on chronic disease management.

Key Takeaways

- Rheumatology involves managing complex, chronic conditions requiring multidisciplinary care.
- Patient empowerment is central to effective treatment.
- Staying current with research enhances clinical practice.

CHAPTER 19

Chapter 19: Dr. Sophie Turner – The Inspiring Ophthalmologist

Dr. Sophie Turner's fascination with ophthalmology began when she witnessed the transformative impact of restoring sight. Growing up in Newcastle, she was inspired by the blend of microsurgical precision and patient interaction involved in eye care. Sophie's journey through medical school and specialty training has been marked by dedication and innovation.

Ophthalmology in the UK faces challenges such as increasing demand from an aging population and managing chronic eye diseases like glaucoma and macular degeneration. Sophie stresses the importance of early detection and integrating new technologies, including laser treatments and advanced imaging, to enhance patient outcomes.

Her clinical practice involves not only surgery but also patient education about eye health and preventative care. Sophie collaborates with optometrists, primary care providers, and low vision support services to provide holistic care.

To maintain balance, she incorporates physical activity, creative hobbies, and mindfulness techniques. Sophie encourages aspiring ophthalmologists to develop fine motor skills, attention to detail, and empathy.

Her story highlights ophthalmology's rewarding blend of precision medicine and compassionate patient care.

Tips & Techniques

- Practice surgical and diagnostic skills with simulation tools.
- Stay updated on advancements in ocular treatments and technology.
- Develop effective communication strategies for patient education.

Action Steps

1. Gain exposure to ophthalmology clinics and surgical theatres.
2. Study common eye diseases and their management.
3. Join ophthalmology societies and attend conferences.

Key Takeaways

- Ophthalmology combines surgical skill with patient-centered care.
- Early detection and technology improve treatment outcomes.
- Balance technical expertise with empathy.

CHAPTER 20

Chapter 20: Dr. Daniel Foster – The Inspirational Plastic Surgeon

Dr. Daniel Foster's journey into plastic surgery was fueled by a blend of artistry, precision, and the desire to restore confidence and function. Growing up in London, Daniel admired the transformative impact reconstructive and aesthetic surgery can have on patients' lives. As an aspiring plastic surgeon myself, his story resonates deeply.

Plastic surgery in the UK faces unique challenges including balancing elective cosmetic procedures with reconstructive demands, navigating NHS resource constraints, and addressing ethical considerations. Daniel highlights the importance of meticulous surgical technique, patient-centred care, and continual learning to stay abreast of innovations.

His work spans from trauma reconstruction to complex microsurgery and cosmetic enhancements, requiring resilience and creativity. Daniel also mentors junior surgeons and advocates for mental health awareness within surgical specialties.

To sustain wellbeing, he practices regular exercise, mindfulness, and maintains a supportive network of colleagues. His journey exemplifies how passion, skill, and empathy combine to create impactful, rewarding careers.

For aspiring plastic surgeons, Daniel's story offers inspiration to pursue excellence, innovation, and compassionate care.

Tips & Techniques

- Hone surgical skills through simulation and supervised practice.
- Develop strong patient communication and ethical decision-making.
- Engage in mentorship and continuous professional development.

Action Steps

1. Seek surgical placements and shadow experienced plastic surgeons.
2. Study anatomy, surgical techniques, and ethical guidelines rigorously.
3. Build resilience through stress management and peer support.

Key Takeaways

- Plastic surgery blends technical precision with artistry and compassion.
- Ongoing learning and mentorship are vital for success.
- Mental wellbeing supports sustainable surgical practice.

BONUS CHAPTER

Bonus Chapter

Academic Pathways to Medicine

Becoming a doctor in the UK involves several academic routes, each designed to prepare you for the demands of medicine. The traditional pathway is through a 5 or 6-year undergraduate medical degree (MBBS or MBChB), often starting straight after A-levels. Graduate entry medicine offers a 4-year accelerated program for those who already hold a degree in a related subject.

Foundation programs provide clinical experience post-graduation before specialty training begins. Other routes include Access to Medicine courses for mature students or those without traditional qualifications. Regardless of the pathway, strong science fundamentals, critical thinking, and a commitment to lifelong learning are essential.

The Importance of Mentors

Mentorship is a cornerstone of medical career development. Mentors provide guidance, encouragement, and valuable insights that textbooks cannot teach. They help navigate challenges, foster professional growth, and open doors to opportunities.

Finding mentors early, whether through medical schools, clinical placements, or professional networks can transform your journey. Remember, mentorship is a two-way relationship built on trust and communication, and as you grow, you too can become a mentor.

Unique Opportunities to Enter Medicine: Conventional & Unconventional

While traditional routes dominate, unique opportunities exist:

- **Healthcare Apprenticeships:** Earn while you learn, gaining practical experience alongside academic study.
- **Degree Apprenticeships:** Combining work with part-time university study, suitable for mature students or those changing careers.
- **International Medical Graduates:** Doctors trained abroad can join the UK system through exams like PLAB or GMC registration.
- **Foundation and Pre-Medical Courses:** Designed to prepare students from diverse backgrounds.
- **Research and Volunteering:** Building experience and networking can open doors to medical schools and specialty training.

Being creative and proactive about your pathway can set you apart and broaden your horizons.

AFFIRMATIONS

Affirmations

When patients step into a doctor's office, they often bring more than symptoms and test results. They bring fears, doubts, and the quiet questions they may not even say out loud: *Will I ever get better? Can I handle this diagnosis? Do I have the strength to keep going?* Medicine addresses the body, but healing often requires something deeper, the belief that we can move forward even in the face of uncertainty.

That is where affirmations come in. Affirmations are not magic words or empty phrases. They are intentional statements that help reframe our thoughts, strengthen resilience, and give voice to hope when fear tries to take over. In the same way a prescription supports physical health, affirmations can support emotional and mental well-being.

This chapter explores how affirmations can be used as a practical tool, not to deny reality, but to ground us in courage, possibility, and self-compassion. Together, we'll look at why affirmations work, how to create them, and how to use them as a daily practice that complements medical care.

Because sometimes, the most healing words are the ones we learn to say to ourselves.

Below are forty affirmations designed to uplift your mood, say them out aloud.

I am capable of achieving excellence in medicine.

Every challenge I face
strengthens my resilience.

My compassion fuels my commitment to healing.

I am continuously growing
as a learner and leader.

I embrace uncertainty as part of my journey.

My voice and perspective
matter in healthcare.

I nurture my wellbeing to
serve others better.

I lead with integrity and empathy.

I welcome feedback as a
tool for improvement.

I am a catalyst for positive
change in medicine.

I balance ambition with self-care.

I build meaningful
connections with patients
and peers.

I am adaptable in a changing healthcare landscape.

I trust my instincts
alongside evidence.

I honour my journey,
including the setbacks.

I inspire others through
my dedication.

I invest in my skills and
knowledge every day.

I am proud to contribute to my community's health.

I celebrate progress over perfection.

I am becoming the doctor
I aspire to be.

Medicine is not just a profession; it's a calling that shapes who we become.

Healing begins with understanding the stories behind every symptom.

In every challenge lies an opportunity to grow stronger and wiser.

Wellbeing is the foundation of effective care, start with yourself.

Leadership in medicine is about listening as much as it is about directing.

Your mindset today will shape
the care you deliver tomorrow.

Compassion and science together create the most powerful medicine.

Dare to ask questions, curiosity is the heart of learning.

The process of hurt, heal, and help is the rhythm of every healer's journey.

Self-care is not selfish; it's essential for sustainable impact.

Innovation thrives where empathy meets expertise.

Your journey is unique, honour it, and let it guide you.

The future of medicine depends on bold, compassionate leaders.

Every patient is a teacher if we choose to learn.

Growth happens outside your comfort zone, embrace discomfort.

To lead others, first learn to lead yourself with kindness.

Success in medicine is built on resilience, not perfection.

Collaboration across
disciplines enhances patient
outcomes.

Believe in your potential even when the path feels uncertain.

Medicine is a journey of continuous discovery, keep exploring

CONCLUSION

Conclusion

The journey to becoming a doctor is undeniably challenging, yet it is filled with moments of profound reward and personal growth. Through the voices of these 20 doctors, we have explored diverse specialties, each with its unique demands and triumphs. Their stories underscore the importance of resilience, empathy, continual learning, and self-care, qualities essential not only to surviving but thriving in medicine.

As you embark or continue on your medical path, remember that every challenge faced is an opportunity to grow, and every patient you care for is a chance to make a lasting difference. Your dedication, curiosity, and compassion will shape the future of healthcare.

FINAL MESSAGE

Final Message

Medicine is a calling that demands the best of us, our intellect, our heart, and our spirit. Let this book inspire you to embrace the journey with confidence and purpose. Whether you find your passion in surgery, mental health, emergency care, or any other field, know that your unique contributions are vital. Keep asking questions, keep learning, and keep caring. Together, we can create a healthier, more compassionate world.

ABOUT THE AUTHOR

About the Author

Yasmine Ben Salmi is a 17-year-old aspiring plastic surgeon with a passion for mental health, wellbeing, self-care, mindset, and leadership within the medical industry. Yasmine is also an author of 12 books and a social entrepreneur. Drawing on her experiences and UK healthcare insights, Yasmine hosts the podcast *Can I Ask You a Question, Doctor?* a platform where she interviews medical professionals to inspire and educate peers on their journey to becoming doctors. She is dedicated to empowering the next generation of healthcare leaders through storytelling, education, and advocacy.

Yasmine founded The Choice Is Yours Publishing House and developed The Choice Is Yours™ program, a proud RSA Fellow, UN Women UK Delegate, Proud contributor alongside my four siblings at the UN SOTF Youth Consultation, multiple award winner, International keynote speaker, moderator, founder of "Can I Ask You A Question Doctor?". Yasmine is a proud member of the Association of Surgeons of Great Britain and Ireland and The British Association of Black Surgeons, which is the UK's largest body of Black surgical professionals.

Yasmine published a scientific article with her mentor Detina Zalli who's a lead professor from Harvard, Oxford and Cambridge: https://oxfordacademy.io/overview-of-reconstructive-plastic-surgery-advantages-and-disadvantages/

KEEP IN TOUCH

Keep in Touch

Thank you for reading *Can I Ask You a Question, Doctor?* I would love to hear your thoughts, experiences, and questions as you pursue your medical journey. Connect with me on social media or through my podcast:

- Podcast: *Can I Ask You a Question, Doctor?*
- Instagram: @AuthorYasmineBenSalmi
- LinkedIn: Yasmine Ben Salmi
- Email: contact@yasminebensalmi.com
- LinkTree: https://linktr.ee/YasmineBenSalmi

Let's keep the conversation going, because every question brings us closer to understanding, healing, and thriving.

NOTES

NOTES

NOTES

NOTES

NOTES

NOTES

NOTES

NOTES

NOTES

NOTES

NOTES

NOTES

NOTES

NOTES

NOTES

NOTES

NOTES

NOTES

NOTES

NOTES

NOTES

www.ingramcontent.com/pod-product-compliance
Lightning Source LLC
LaVergne TN
LVHW051237080426
835513LV00016B/1631